# The Red Strings Between

## Rachael Li Ming Chong

VERVE
POETRY PRESS
BIRMINGHAM

PUBLISHED BY VERVE POETRY PRESS
https://vervepoetrypress.com
mail@vervepoetrypress.com

*All rights reserved*
© 2025 Rachael Li Ming Chong
The right of Rachael Li Ming Chong to be identified as author of this work has been asserted in accordance with section 77 of the Copyright, Designs and Patents Act 1988.

No part of this work may be reproduced, stored or transmitted in any form or by any means, graphic, electronic, recorded or mechanical, without the prior written permission of the publisher.

FIRST PUBLISHED JUNE 2025

Printed and bound in the UK
by Imprint Digital, Exeter

ISBN: 978-1-913917-61-6

# CONTENTS

| | |
|---|---|
| It Will Surface Simultaneous | 4 |
| Hi-Spy Viewing Machine | 5 |
| Spectral Finish | 7 |
| In the Absence of Paperclips | 9 |
| Kumamoto Rain | 10 |
| In the Corridor Connecting the *Onsen* and *Tatami* Lounge | 11 |
| Oshima Giant | 12 |
| Spectroscopy | 14 |
| Papaw | 15 |
| No Room for Tupperware Ghosts | 16 |
| Our red string criss-crosses continents. | 17 |
| Inwangsan on Pause | 18 |
| We Exchange Blood on Bark for the Best Fruit | 19 |
| Capillary Motion | 20 |
| You Call It Your Secret Garden | 21 |
| Whether to Tug When You Don't Know What's at the End | 23 |
| Having Lost the Place to Land | 24 |
| Learning to Succeed | 27 |
| Fukushima, Matsuura | 29 |

*Acknowledgements*

# It Will Surface Simultaneous

Follow the belly of the valley until your cheeks
mildew with moss and we'll be there
dislodging clouds from woodland debris.
It will surface simultaneous.
Pennies, pendants, the red macintosh rising
like the lipping of milk, the hems of sleeves curled over
with altitude sickness.
Torn pages from maps wrinkled in exasperation
for all the roads we didn't trace with our fingers.
Bus tickets, birthday chestnuts in their jackets,
your name spun frail in calligraphy
straining to hold your place at the table.
Is this what we came for? To wipe storm spit
from our unslept faces, to pocket his grandfather's key
the one that rotates strictly clockwise
paralysing locks in its wake?
Send your lens skyward so it shows
the waterways in our neighbourhoods, until
the roots of their eddies tangle in a vortex ache.
One day in a puddle you notice it, familiar.
The stirring of water - the gentle murmur
of all the turbulence from under.

# Hi-Spy Viewing Machine

           The ocean        zoomed in
                            seven times
               looks       exactly like the ocean
                            you lament
             roving      your hire eyes
for signs of an earth
              where      banana leaves
         substitute     surfboards
      jellyfish pitch    into four-man tents
the crest of a wave  can be sugared
                            then shaped
         with sand      buckets
                            a cake
                            for your neighbour's wedding.

I spun it one-eighty   once
to see your laughter  echoing off the brow
of the Japanese Alps

                          *Never Let Me Go* rolled
in your back pocket

                          final page
                          anaemic
                          from re-reading
         you'd been
              riding      funiculars
towards the break    of the sun

           don't get me      wrong

                 there       too
            were signs
                             of weathering
       pockets padded        with last year's receipts
       and rubbed-worn       totems -
                             though that was when
the soil of your tread
             vibrated        urgently
                             to breed planets

            when hope
                             was handwoven

                             when the ocean
            zoomed in        seven times
            did not look     exactly
            like the ocean.

# Spectral Finish

Today the paintwork of the 06:54 train popped
also the blushing ear tips of asparagus
pigeons and their burly chests beaming iridescence
wild bluebell heads (staring intently at their stems)
red onions with and without their paper skins

and in their radiance
surrounding objects celebrated
and/or grew envious for attention
mimicked their wavelengths
so it glinted from the lids of yoghurt pots
refracted off pavement stones
onto the buckles of our shoes
and it was there ruminating
between lines of newspaper print
until the pupils of all the commuters
glowed like cherried moons

and the trains didn't mind
and the pigeons delighted
and the asparagus and the bluebells
and the red onions skinned and skinless
concentrated brighter
so others might join

a collective to project
not further just really to the interiors
where the rings of trees
and the crumb structure of cake
could see the world of indigo

so everyone would know
to look to the morning sun
behind its paper-screen mist
see it thread suspended droplets of water
and remember
that in the curvature of light
richard of york gave battle in vain

and continued bruising after death

# In the Absence of Paperclips

I plunge my hand into a bucket of tadpoles. Tangled in my hair,
a pinecone waiting to self-implode. The sun sets into aspic jelly.

I squat, hover over the pavement like charged static. *Da Capo
al Coda*, thoughts on rinse-spin loop.  A flavourless gumball

and all its jaw ache. When the construction workers turn their backs
I throw jigsaw-pieced regrets into the cement mixer. They fold

into concentric circles. I know where it goes. Yesterday was the vernal equinox
and all the apples, onions, eggs throbbed in anticipated halves.

I declare my name over and over, seal it in glass jars in multiples of three
to counter future jinxes. I dial all the landline numbers I know off by heart,

none connect through. My fingerprints are disintegrated road maps
coffee-glued to the base of your glove compartment. You call me your *favourite*,

you pencil in cartoon eyes on my wallpaper. They follow me to my study
and see my corners folded over. They know where I go.

You draw circles on my back, tell me they are triangles. I rearrange
nerve endings to make this true. There is another hemisphere

where I stare at the oil splatters on the backsplash
and their constellations spell out a different face.

# Kumamoto Rain

The rain began to fall. Tentatively at first, a cat's paw testing soft uneven ground. And then ferociously, at full force - cascades of heavy, frothing sheets. They ran. Bolted aimlessly, with their backs arched and palms canopying their eyes - as if their rounded posture and interlaced fingers would shield them from the downpour, as if running meant they stood a chance of outsmarting the rain. A nearby shopkeeper slid shut their front door, a rogue taxi-driver avoided eye contact and drove determinedly away. They felt an anchoring towards the earth in each strained step of their sprint. They slowed down. Stopped, simultaneously. Stretched out their arms - in submission first - then, in acceptance of the rain. Here they were - lost amidst a monsoon in a strange and unpredictable land; together, drenched, and unshakably alive.

# In the Corridor Connecting the *Onsen* and *Tatami* Lounge

I anticipate the wait.
The smell of sulphur, chlorine and wet carpet
as I consider which flavour of yoghurt probiotic.

I pretend to move with purpose.
Inspect the fire policy notice above the plastic
chair, plot out an escape route with my finger.

Like the landscapes holding us
I trace impatience in these walls.
Matter refusing permanence.

That corner of peeling paint
jagged chip of magnolia
its contours somehow familiar

and the vending machine
spits out a hum caught
between a lullaby and a groan

for recognition. I pin phantom
name tags on all the objects
to coax them into holding

their position in this place where
I am particles of myself
and you are all the spaces between.

# Oshima Giant

We were the only guests. Hostel on a hill, hunched
over woodlands in the Shikoku night.
No mixing of sexes, the hosts insist, thumbs
split, pointing towards bedroom quarters at
opposite ends. And so I mouth: instant ramen
party in the kitchen at ten. You negate to participate in this.
You prefer question marks, exiting quietly,
discarded keys and phone - an exhibit
in how to run away curated on the duvet of your bed.
Our friend, the enigma, we nervously whisper.

You stand on the hostel steps.
Lovesick on a hill, you see her handstand in every tree
the shifting weight, the boned wrists,
the pointed archway as her legs split,
one leads to a story you are tired of re-reading.
And so you headline the alternate.
You descend the forest of *taiheiyo* evergreens
a soundtrack in how to run away
reverberates from cicada wing to cicada wing.
Our friend, the lionhearted, we admiringly whisper.

Your face is filmed over with broken webs.
Bottom of the hill, you tightrope
the painted line of the road, the earth levelling
at each step. You reach an *izakaya*.
Another life split behind paper screens,

laughter rattles through the door, rises
to the moon like floating debris.
You blow dust from a quiet piece of flesh,
a narrative in how to run away translated
in broken Japanese.
Our friend, the pioneer, we pass on the whisper

a positive wave, ionised air
to the chopsticks of strangers.

# Spectroscopy

That's all it took - the bridge of a yellow spark
between two electrodes to conjure up the ghost
of a suspended yolk in a vacuum of shell.

And now we can diagnose the make-up of stars.

That's how I knew to trace you
in the powdered residue of sleep
stormed up on sweated-in sheets
the first absent autumn.

It was red - *hóngbāo* red - the same red of your run
towards our departing car when we'd drop you home
teaching us a goodbye   ought to be chased
ought to be stretched, spun from its centre
until it orbits each iteration of clenched fist
the elastic scattering of laughter.

It's the lightwaves we emit that speak
the syllables of our atomic structures.
I learned to map mine in the confusion
of your eyes that day you did not run.

My outline refracted in your ruby pupils
a silhouette stretched further. My body
in shades of a landscape painted over.

# Papaw

Your skin sags with the absence of fat and muscle. Spiderweb on bone. My skin is stretched and groaning. Your day is yawning, curled up in the corner by the woodfire. Mine erupts with a multitude of other. How unfair it is for me to sit next to you - the stench of life on my apple-bite breath. When your loved-ones leave, you say, 'I'm afraid'. I offer up my hand, a weak gesture - as if my tendons could counter-tremble. Later, we pass on a clue folded up in a piece of paper. You study what it could mean - sample its flavour. The pause unfurling to a sky. No introductions - you exchange nods in recognition, throw out fly-lines together. Or is that a tossed football arching over your shared horizon? Contrails whisk the stale air, condense into nests around our shoulders, which we absent-mindedly shrug off.

# No Room for Tupperware Ghosts

Your hair grows six inches per year.
So I measure mine and divide by six; this hair
has nearly never known you.

We lose all our outer skin cells
over the course of a month, so here
I am, sitting on the park bench

willing my epidermis to advance its millions,
a swirl of invisible me awaiting
a new surface area

a fresh container
of blood, fat, bones
no room for Tupperware ghosts.

The branch of the tree droops low, reaching out
for the soil of its roots - let's say
in autumn it was anchored

by an abundance of fruit, so I can repeat
*apple-laden* out loud - this mantra rising, trembling
the highest twig in the sun.

# Our red string criss-crosses continents.

Migrating swallows and cargo planes get tangled up in our string, fragments of meteor too. Our red string pierces cumulus clouds, is buried under sand and manure, skims glacier lakes, travels along electricity pylons of sprawling cities, spans the peaks of mountains. Himalayan monks construct pulley systems with our string, use it to deliver gift baskets of berries. Gibbons zipline through. Our red string dives in and out of text message ghosts and pieces of time capsule. Follows the looped cursive of words not yet written. Races light waves. Satellites the moon. Has gone through phases where it's dyed itself purple, sometimes green. Will roll around in peppermint sugar, deny it's a string altogether. Our red string lines airport waiting lounges, cast iron pans in my kitchen. Pins itself up like bunting. Catches eyelashes and parachute seeds, in springtime sprouts patches of clover. Has stretches that smell of green tea, sulphur, stale cabin, pine. Tie our red string to a tin can, press it to your ear and hear waterfalls, wheels spinning at seventy five miles per hour. The inhalation of breath before every goodbye. Your end of red string has already met mine. See it entwine, its braid running like backbone through Kyūshū, volcano-dipped and calcified. Our red string knows its story has evolved beyond intersection, that narrative swells in its endings: how it follows me to the quiet places and still oscillates with a tug, reciprocal, bee wings on my finger. How it startles the still air with tremors. Transmitting ferocious waves of you.

# Inwangsan on Pause

Pagoda
sprouting mountain-side.
*Hōju* gleams
on a spire.
A teardrop shed by city
sky, a winter scar.
If you stand
still enough
a snowglobe forms
and you're the centrepiece.

# We Exchange Blood on Bark for the Best Fruit

There is dust in the air. Unsure of where to settle.
Clouds stand milky and coagulate tartly
and the leaves on the birch tree loiter, prophesying
the wind's shift. We are restless at these times.
A film of sweat fuses our skins to the leathers
of sofa, our metamorphosis into furniture.

The lawn mowers spit out the heads of overgrowth
and we hide the outline of silhouettes made out
on the horizon in the heat pockets of compost.

To be chewed up and reclaimed fertile.

Find us, one more time. In the hitches of knotweed,
in the centre of orange flower that has no name
because the language is unknown
so there is no name. And along the towpath
the dust selects its place: on the sloes that ripen
between thorns in the hedgerows. To blanket
the blue-black defiance of astringent berry.

They say early winter frost is the time
to harvest, so the bonds in its skin will weaken,
so its skin will break, will permeate in a bath of liquor.

They say you can imitate first frost in the freezer.
Pressed between index and thumb
that critical moment before splitting

still resisting in its armour of powder cape.

# Capillary Motion

My ancestors peeped over a pyramid of freckled pears,
through smoke ribbons of agarwood to witness
my graduation to words with more permanence.

No more pencil - a fountain pen, gifted from the family shop;
they *gānbēied* raucously at the promise tint in its trail,
Roman letters scrawled over borders Ah Tai Kong never

crossed. It came with a bottle of Quink, souped up with sweat
wrung from Popo's neck towel and sirens circled
along the glass rim. They shook it wildly to infuriate the ink.

It fermented tartly in its cartridge and surged out
across paper lines, brittle boned *hanzi* skittling
in its wake: *won't, can't, shouldn't, couldn't; pierce, piece,*

*priest, belief; knock, knee, knowledge, knife;*
a continuous line of cursive trans-continental ghosts
would tug upon, nodding as it held its place.

In science class I unscrewed the bottom shell to marvel
at its reservoir glow in front of the fluorescent fixtures.
I learned how to lemon-soak my words without applying heat.

The split of the nib - it grew tired, warped ink
to a manuscript of blots increasingly only I could decipher.
See now my hands, they linger. Waiting,

for the gasp before the mark, the flow of liquid into narrow spaces.

# You Call It Your Secret Garden

Little landing strip in front
of the cobbled wall, behind
the quarry site fence,
vegetables take-off casually.

Studded star of courgette flower.
Bean shoots and their tendril
curls around scaffold poles: the tender
fleshing of bamboo skeleton.

And in the corner, joyful bursts
of shark fin melon. Jade green
rind with mottled blush,
water-coloured then rain-washed.

You slice thick wedges with
your cleaver, it softens in *ikan bilis* broth,
disintegrates to a debris
of butter seeds and thread-plump pulp,

our source of perennial warmth
in communal dips of porcelain spoon.

Your master stock is a galaxy
rarely stirred. Mulled in ours, we struggle
to define its flavour - white radish and bone
float up to surface, it prefers to emulsify under.

We've caught glimpses of its composition
in your margin scribble: fermented
mustard greens, blood of beheaded
chicken, reclaimed crusts of *kaya* toast

scavenged from the floor
of next door's *kopitiam*.

Each element you've found pairings
to balance raw taste back
into palatable water, an expert
in alchemy on the translucence of soups.

Still - your stock eddies, continues
to thicken. Is it the other secret garden?

We see her wandering around the conifer trees,
smoothing back the earth
over each footprint, slipping behind
the shed holding the freezer chest.

You follow her there.
Her red purse urgent and full
of seeds, she spills them
into your outstretched palms.

We hear the echoing whispers
when the soup-fat pips burst
under our teeth, with each slurped
strand of shark fin melon.

*I have smuggled these across oceans
and your soil is full of stones.*

# Whether to Tug When You Don't Know What's at the End

There's a red string tied to my ankle.
It's been there since the first beat.
Ah Nai told me to always keep an eye
of its position in the horizon, to smooth
its strands regularly with petroleum jelly.
*Of course, your grandfather is tied
to mine,* she says, casting off
a knitting line, refusing to look me in the eye.
I thought of my childhood, weaving in
and out of trees not caring about the tangles.
And now, every flash of red makes my heart seize.
Red, in the accidental faces of seaside rocks.
Red, cracked out of spherical eggs,
expanding in milk foam hearts.
The red of the telephone wire in the forest
that channels small talk to the dead.
His sundrenched skin, red.
*Life is the ebb and flow, the pull and tug.*
But what about the fray and the slack,
the red between my legs?
The first trauma, separating myself
from my mother?
*At least that was a clean slice.*

# Having Lost the Place to Land

*after Zarina Hashmi*

I thought I found it.
The front elevation - stripped dimensions,
windows with plus sign grilles
that blinked through drawing curtains:
*There's potatoes roasting in the oven.*
*This is where you return.*

Except it had no chimney. So I drew one.
With charming mismatched bricks
a Canadian goose weathervane
nailed to its rim and trailing smoke puffs
in descending size which I followed
like stepping stones in the sky
though stepping stones are supposed to lead
to the other side - and these just petered out.
(well that's on me)

It began well, this minimal life.
I chose my ideal toaster.
Started a collection of turtle neck sweaters.
My bed was a jetty defying
the undertow of the laminate floor.

A liquid's shape is dictated
by the shape of its container.
I discovered mine was so wide
everyone broke their necks
whenever they tried to dive in.
Playing lifeguard, it was tiring.

So I clicked my heels three times.
Found myself
on another continent
surrounded by guava trees.
At first didn't speak the language
so played menu roulette.
Chatted up shepherds via dictionary.
And when mosquito bites ceased
to make me itch I thought
okay - this time I've arrived?

Other parts disagreed.

My tongue kept floating off.
I had to learn how to cook
*kolo mein* and *jook* to convince it to stay.
My eyes insisted in panning for gold
in the gutters. I self-diagnosed.
The search result said: *You're afflicted
with the opposite of motion sickness.
Choose a focal point that's kinetic.*
I fucked up all the compasses
with magnets. Followed the sun
with a folding deck chair
tucked under my arm.
Intently studied meteor showers.

Learned to trace the fragments
back to their radiant point
the meeting of parallel paths.

Trace the radiant point
back to a constellation
in contempt of its webbing.

Trace the constellation
back to five star nodes
then the darkness between.

Trace the darkness between
back to four bold lines
a room's negative space.

Trace the negative space
back to a scribble of arteries
from Mama and Popo
braid thick into blanket
the birthright of daughters
I wrap around my shoulders
that is enough to keep me warm
now that I've shed
these bricks from my bones.

# Learning to Succeed

How could it be - the corridor lining
your classroom, the green wire gate,
the store selling boiler parts - should slip
from the default architecture of your sleep?

You sift through scrolls of blueprints only to find
blocky accented lines, bricks and mortar
like molars overcrowding, your rib gaps widening
to expose a window of vital organ.

Your feet no longer fit your footprints, instead
practise how to redistribute the weight
into each stride, draw a map for all the places
you can stockpile steady pockets of breath.

Chicken bone.　　　　Bus stop.
　　　　　　Pothole.　　　Leaf.
The wind crossing your cheeks
will speed up further east.

Ask your seconds to sunbathe.
The pencils in your drawer are ready
to shed their cedar, the post-it notes dream
of their moment, heroic, to prevent milk-less tea.

The traffic lights entertain themselves along the A40,
and next to the acorns, sisters
will plant piano keys, extrapolate
where the tarmac might meet your feet.

So whatever the order of your forward:
back, forth, sideways, pause, forth, back -
for you, a cascade of broken chords
in each translated step.

# Fukushima, Matsuura

Do you remember the gravel-rattle
of the grey dashboard, the way
our shoulders swayed on loom-pin bends?

We braked abruptly mid-road, flung wide
the dented doors, raced out towards the
edge of the rice paddy folds.

Look - how the fields cascade, stretch
from peak right down to coastal hem,
jumbled charmingly; a staircase, crooked,

black kites buttering the canopy air, they hum
along the rim of the singing bowl
dipped sonorous in the sky, one-by-

one, they plunge, meteoric, dot
-to-dotting the terraces parabolic
until the papery collapse of their lungs;

their bellies brush the dust of the sea.
You asked: is this how our memories here
will come to pass – in a single, haunting

swoop? That was the day the
sky was turning - a pale and milky
sour. I was sprawled out on *tatami*,

lattice scored cheeks, thumbing
down loose *igusa* threads. The glassware
shook Richter three, but perhaps

that was the rumbling through scenes of
our divergence, or was it my mouth
breaking the surface - which then all fragmented,

powder into air. Outside, the harvest frogs
were in chorus, so I released
my fingernails from palm lines,

clenched in tight to hold home in:
flow, bloodstream, flow
with their loud and joyful croaking.

ACKNOWLEDGEMENTS

Many thanks to the following publications where some of these poems, or versions of them, have first appeared: *Poetry Archive, Modron Magazine, Public Sector Poetry, From the Silence of the Stacks: New Voices Rise 5* (London Library), *Swapping the Present for a Future – The Verve Anthology of Beginnings* (VERVE Poetry Press), *Where We Find Ourselves* (Arachne Press).

Many thanks to Creative Future for granting me a Writers' Award, and resources to help me develop this pamphlet. Thank you especially to Victoria MacKenzie for your insightful feedback on my manuscript, and to Matt Freidson and Nina Mingya Powles for your generosity and time.

Many thanks to Cecilia Knapp for your guidance and kindness, and for motivating me to continue writing.

Many thanks to my writing communities for helping me to nurture my poetic practice - particularly the Poetry Coven, and the London Library Poets '24.

Many thanks to Stuart Bartholomew at Verve Poetry Press for your editorial leadership and giving these poems a home.

Monumental thanks to the following (and many others) for your inspiration, support, encouragement and love:
Betty Chong, Peter Chong, Troy Lewis, Emiko Lewis-Chong, Kaito Lewis-Chong, Daniel Chong, Joanne Murray, Leo Murray-Chong, Nathan Chong, Elizabeth Chong, Sukong, Chip Lewis, Masako Meade, Patrick Meade, Dawson Roy Lewis III, Rena Han, Cory Lewis, Navneet Desai, Anne-Marie Choong, Maryam Intisar, Jodie Curran, Michelle Yip, Gagandeep Grewal, Eunice Chow, Bindu Joseph, Blessy Joseph, Hardip Biring, Bhavik Bhatt, Maiuran Vijendra, Amandeep Phull, Rola Harb, Dipa Pindoria, Marline Shaheen, Haydar Shah, Laura Webb, Kumiko Yamada, Lynn Rusk, Eleanor Fulham, Patrick William Smith.

ABOUT THE AUTHOR

**Rachael Li Ming Chong** is a poet and teacher, based in London. She is a winner of The Poetry Archive's WordView 2021 Competition and the 2023 Creative Future Writers' Poetry Award. She is an alumna of the HarperCollins Author Academy and the London Library Emerging Writers Programme. She holds advanced degrees in education from UCL and the University of Cambridge, and has been awarded grants from the Royal Society of Literature and Let Teachers SHINE for independent development projects targeting educational attainment in literature and mathematics. *The Red Strings Between* is her debut poetry pamphlet.

*For Emiko and Kaito*